Dazzledance

for Heather

I have an eye of silver,
I have an eye of gold,
I have a tongue of reed-grass
    and a story to be told.

I have a hand of metal,
I have a hand of clay,
I have two arms of granite
    and a song for every day.

I have a foot of damson,
I have a foot of corn,
I have two legs of leaf-stalk
    and a dance for every morn.

I have a dream of water,
I have a dream of snow,
I have a thought of wildfire
    and a harp-string long and low.

I have an eye of silver,
I have an eye of gold,
I have a tongue of reed-grass
    and a story to be told.

Climbing the World

Heading home, the faces
of the passengers opposite
are reflected dark blue
in the late night train windows.

I doze, my daughter yawns.

The head of the sleeping man
next to me lolls about like a puppet's.
His paperback slips from his lap
and falls onto the orange peel
he discarded before falling asleep.

He wakes in time to get off at Sevenoaks.

I pick up the book, brush the peel off the jacket.
It's *The Diary of a Young Girl: Anne Frank,*
the '97 Penguin edition, due back
at Paddington Library by 13 Dec.
I start reading the foreword

. . . Anne Frank kept a diary . . .

Her father, Otto Frank, edited her diaries
after she was dead.
I see him crying at the typewriter.

My daughter is 27.
We have great times together.
She is my friend and I love her.
Even in a train's harsh light she is very beautiful.
She is climbing the world.

Anne and Otto Frank
have taught me how to tell you this.

I shall now return the sleeping man's
book to Paddington Library.

Careful With That, You Might Break It

See what I've found.

Oh be careful with that,
it's so delicate, it could easily break.

If you take it in your hands gently
you can hold it
close up to your eyes.

It's a bit hazy on the outside,
but if you wait for it to turn,
here and there you can see right through
and then you'll be really amazed!

Gently now, even though it looks solid enough,
you'd be surprised at just how flimsy it is.
Look there. Can you see the big blue bits?
I remember being so fascinated with them
that I wanted to touch them.

But you're not allowed to do that.
If you did, The High says you might damage it
because there's some protective coating
or gas or something surrounding the whole thing
and if that gets damaged, it could be serious.
What do you suppose the green bits are?

That's it, just let it rest in your palm.
Watch how it spins of its own accord.
Have you spotted the brown areas?
No, you mustn't touch the little white thing
going round it, The High says it's very important too,
a force or influence or balance perhaps.
Let's leave it now, careful, don't forget it's so very
  fragile.

It's name?
The High call it *Earth*.
Some say it's a sad place.

Scottish Haiku

A bonny Ayrshire
chews the cud on Ben Nevis,
noo *that's* a high coo!

A Minute to Midnight

**A minute to midnight
and all is still.**

For example, these are things that are still:
ornaments, coins, lamp-posts,
the cooker, Major Clark's Home for old folk
(just opposite our house, which is also still),
the newsagent's, a hut, soap, tractors,
freshly ironed trousers draped over the chair.

**A minute to midnight
and all is still
except for the things that are moving.**

Like, for example,
rivers, clouds, leaves, flags,
creaky windmills, lungs, birds' feathers,
digital clocks, grass, the wind,
non-sleeping animals (especially wolves),
planet Earth, the moon, satellites in space,
toenails (well they grow don't they),
videos that are set to record
programmes in the middle of the night,
washing lines,
mobiles above babies' cots –
and babies' eyelids, they always flicker.

Driving at Night with My Dad

Open the window,
the cool summer night swooshes in.
My favourite music playing loud.

2 a.m. – summer's midnight –
neither of us can sleep
so we go for a night drive.

Stars crowd the sky
and twinkle at us in code.
Out headlights reply in light language.

A fox crosses, red and grey,
and arches under a fence:
rabbits run and a farm cat's eyes
catch our beam.
She stares at us for a second of stretched time . . .
. . . her eyes two new coins.

Through villages that are asleep,
past farms that are warm,
past houses that are dreaming,
under trees that are resting,
past birds that have no flight, no song.

I sense I am in some other country
where day, time, people no longer matter.
In this huge dark,
through the somewhere and the nowhere
of this uninhabited world,
I feel safe and secure
driving at night with my dad.

The Mysteries of Nature
or Globular Bunkular My Duck Has Sunkular

Nature poems are popular
but seldom very jocular
but this one is spectacular
because it's quite funicular

Let's take a country walkular
through fields that are rusticular
look through your binocular
there's an eagle and a hawkular

The hedgerow in particular
is a home so very insular
for creatures shaped triangular
or even semi-circular

You may come across a spookular
in the forest deep and darkular
a sharp stab in your jugular
means you've met up with Count Dracular

By the church that looks so secular
there is a pond where you'll find duckular
this one doesn't quackular
since it argued with a truckular

I see by the town clockular
that time is passing quickular
I think I need a breakular
too much nature makes you sickular

If . . .

If ships sailed on the motorway
   and potato crisps were blue,
if football boots were made of silk
   and a lamp-post wore a shoe.

If motorbikes ran upwards
   and milk floats really floated,
if beds were full of dinosaurs
   and peas were sugarcoated.

If flies wore bomber-jackets
   and eggs laid little chickens,
if spacemen had a panther each
   and insects studied Dickens.

If babies' prams were motorized
   and you listened to your conscience,
if your brain was working properly
   you wouldn't read this nonscience.

Low Owl

a univocalic*

Cold morn: on fork of two o'clock
owl's hoot flows from hood of wood.

Owl's song rolls from blood to brood,
owl's hoot loops on to top of town roofs,
owl's song swoops on strong doors.

Owl's slow whoop – long, forlorn –
soft flood of moon song.

**a poem which uses only one of the five vowels:
in this case the letter 'o'.*

Castle to be Built in the Woods

Choose a wood.

Make a clearing
near a stream.

Dig a moat.
Make it deep, wide.
Fill it with water. One bridge only.

Lay solid foundations for your castle.
Then build strong buttresses, stout keeps
and tall towers with crenellations
around the high battlements.

Make sure your castle has servants such as
clerks, tailors, nurses, messengers,
damsels, brewers, and a barber.
You will need to lay down stores
of food, wine, wax, spices and herbs.

An airy church inside the castle grounds
and a dark dungeon deep below ground
will mean that you can have
Heaven and Hell at your fingertips.
Don't forget to stock your arsenal with
swords, daggers, lances, shields, battle-axes, etc.

Fire arrows at anyone who tries to
attack your castle. Build murder-holes
so that you can drop missiles and stones
on the heads of your enemies.
If you catch spies, lock them in
the smallest, narrowest, smelliest room.
Act ruthlessly. Behead people, frequently.

Hide treasure in a very secret part of the castle.
Lock a beautiful princess in the tower.
Force your fiercest dragon to guard both of these.
Nominate a knight who will fight your battles
so that you are never injured or endangered.
Employ a storyteller to make up tall tales
and ghost stories about your castle.
Marry someone and he can be the king.

The Divers and the Dolphins

Ah, just look at them,
aren't they beautiful?

So graceful, so sleek
as they swim around the boat –

poking their snouts up
to break the surface,

then diving straight down,
blowing bubbles all the time.

And look at all their different colours.
I'll bet they could fetch things.

I've even seen one
dive deep down to a wrecked ship.

Look at its oval eye, so large, so glassy.
And listen; I'm sure they're communicating.

Not 'talking' as we know it,
but they're certainly intelligent.

Strange how those land-leggers feel they have
to dive underwater from time to time.

Constant, Constant Little Light

*A 21st-century version of Jane Taylor's poem 'THE STAR',
now universally known as the nursery rhyme 'Twinkle,
twinkle little star'*

Constant, constant little light,
catch my eye in darkest night.
What can speed so fast, so high,
laser like across the sky?

When the sleepy sun has set
and the night has cast her net.
It's then your orbit forms a ring,
round the earth a song to sing.

Constant, constant little light,
I know you're a satellite.

Cruising, spinning, seldom seen,
beaming pictures to our screens.
Weather-watching, tracking storms,
plotting maps and all life-forms.

Scanning, spying from above,
are you hawk or are you dove?
Silent, stealthy space age Thor,
armed with weapons for a real star war.

From your tiny, silver glow,
who can tell what wrongs may flow.
But for now I hold you bright,
constant, constant little light.

Constant, constant little light,
I know you're a satellite.

Guzzling Jelly with Giant Gorbelly

Who's that swilling soup
made from mouldy mutton?
It's the giant's little son, Gorbelly Button.

Fancy watching telly? Not on your Nelly!
We'd rather guzzle jelly with Giant Gorbelly!

Who's that gobbling garlic
and a grilled lamb chop?
It's the giant's sweet daughter, Gorbelly Flop.

Fancy watching telly? Not on your Nelly!
We'd rather guzzle jelly with Giant Gorbelly!

Who's that chewing chicken
and feeding on a fish cake?
It's the giant's grumpy daddy, Gorbelly Ache.

Fancy watching telly? Not on your Nelly!
We'd rather guzzle jelly with Giant Gorbelly!

Who's that pecking pork
and scoffing half a calf?
It's the giant's tickly mummy, Gorbelly Laugh.

Fancy watching telly? Not on your Nelly!
We'd rather guzzle jelly with Giant Gorbelly!

Who's that biting beef
bought from Marks & Spanser.
It's the giant's darling wife, Gorbelly Dancer.

Fancy watching telly? Not on your Nelly!
We'd rather guzzle jelly with Giant Gorbelly!

When Mr and Mrs Gorbelly Go Shopping

When **Gorbelly the Giant** and his wife
    Gorbelly Dancer
go shopping at the
SuperHyperMegaMarket,
they carry monstrous, megalithic, monumental
plastic bags and they buy

ten thousand **Titanic-sized** tins
of processed people

countless **colossal** cans of baked beings

a billion **bulky** bottles of *humanade*

piles of paunchy packets of **folk fingers**

hugely ginormous jars of pickled persons

a ***hundred herculean*** cartons of children chunks

twenty a-plenty podgy portions of ***pensioner***
    pieces

six thousand strapping slices of **grilled grown-ups.**

The Gorbellies have a shopping list
as long as an airport runway.
They use a jumbo jet as a shopping trolley.
On their way home they often pick up
a theme park or a fairground as a present

for their little son . . . **Gorbelly Button!**

Gorbelly Button and his Daddy Gorbelly

Gorbelly Button and his Daddy Gorbelly
live in a house called Shimble Shamshelly
which is just down the road, not far from Dalmelly
where the kids are sweet but the babies are smelly

It's a very large house is Shimble Shamshelly
with its huge living room and its widescreen telly
and their housekeeper's name is Katie Ann Kelly
but she smells rather strange, like a soaking wet welly

Now eat up your food, says Daddy Gorbelly
you must drink the sea and eat beaches that are shelly
eat up your sharks, your fishes made of jelly
for you'll want to be like me and have a ginormous
belly

Gannet Diving

Beak,
harpoon, or cocktail stick.

Neck,
brushed yellowy snowbridge.

Wings,
a flash of glassy light,
tipped black as school socks.

Tail,
a trailing shirt-tail,
freshly ironed.

Dives,
a white arrowhead
speeding from silk blue sky
to ice blue water.

Rises,
from white frothy broth
with wriggling silver prize.

Gulps,
goes for gold.

Leisure Centre, Pleasure Centre

You go through plate-glass doors
with giant red handles,
into light that's as bright
as a million candles.
The chlorine smells,
the whole place steaming,
the kids are yelling
and the kids are screaming.

Watch them
wave jump
dive thump
cartwheel
free wheel
look cute
slip chute
toe stub
nose rub
in the leisure centre, pleasure centre.

Sporty people laugh and giggle
folk in swimsuits give a wiggle.
Kids are in the café busy thinking
if they can afford some fizzy drinking.
In the changing rooms
wet folk shiver

It's hard to get dressed
when you shake and shiver.

And we go
breast stroke
back stroke
two stroke
big folk
hair soak
little folk
eye poke
in the leisure centre, pleasure centre.

And now we're driving back home
fish 'n' chips in the car,
eyes are slowly closing
but it's not very far.
Snuggle wuggle up in fresh clean sheets
a leisure centre trip
is the best of treats

because you can
keep fit
leap sit
eat crisps
do twists
belly flop
pit stop
fill up
with 7-Up
get going
blood flowing
look snappy
be happy
in the leisure centre, pleasure centre.

Ettykett

My mother knew a lot about manners,
she said you should never slurp;
you should hold your saucer firmly,
and not clang your teeth on the curp.

My father knew nothing about manners,
all he could do was slurp;
and when I can't find a rhyming word,
I set about making them urp.

Instructions for Giants

Please do not step on swing parks, youth clubs,
    cinemas or skate parks.
Please flatten all schools!

Please do not eat children, pop stars, TV soap actors,
    kind grannies who give us 50p.
Please feel free to gobble up dentists and teachers
    any time you like!

Please do not block out the sunshine.
Please push all rain clouds over to France.

Please do not drink the public swimming pool.
Please eat all cabbage fields, vegetable plots
    and anything green that grows in the
        boring countryside!

Please do not trample kittens, lambs or other baby
    animals.
Please take spiders and snakes, ants and beetles home
    for your pets.

Please stand clear of jets passing.
Please sew up the ozone layer.
Please mind where you're putting your big feet –
and no sneaking off to China when we're playing
    hide-and-seek!

How Captain Angel Came into Being

(for Jill Doe)

Long away and far,
there once was a silver age of harmony
between All-the-Skies and All-the-Earths.

High was high, low was low,
and on a day of weather,
much like the weather of today,
puffy clouds parted and a golden sunray
shone through to form a lift-shaft of light.

And an angel slid down to be among us.

The angel became rock, too steady.
The angel became sea, too wavy.
The angel became snowflake, too chilled.
The angel became rain, too damp.
The angel became feather, too tickly.
The angel became air, so wispy. Just right.

A little girl somewhere drew a big breath
. . . *aaaaaahhhhhhhimp* . . .
and inhaled the angel-in-air.
It was not unpleasant, even though
it felt as if she had swallowed
a rubber doll or a small yellow dinghy.

Girl became angel, angel became girl.
Girl-Angel needed a name.
'Take the next word we speak,' said Angel-Girl.

On the television quiz show
the quiz lady asked, 'On the Starship Enterprise,
what rank was held by James T. Kirk?'

'CAPTAIN!' yelled Girl-Angel and Angel-Girl
both at the same start-of-time,
both in the same end-of-time voice.

'Captain Angel' took flight.

How Captain Angel Learned to Sing

It was or it was not, on a low day, a day above all days,
that Captain Angel was flying high, listening to the
     radio.

It was no ordinary music that was playing,
it was a music of verse-paintings. A glass music.

'I want to sing!' cried Captain Angel suddenly,
'to enrich this poor world with a beauty cold as Saturn.'

Inspired, Captain Angel changed course and flew
straight to the Music School. It was closed on a Sunday.

Annoyed and disappointed, Captain Angel sat down
on the grass and looked up at the whirling sky.

A sack of grey cloud was travelling west:
dog-like face, torpedo body, flippered. A seal-cloud.

'That's it! The seals will teach me to sing.'
A speedy lift-off left a smoking burn in the grass.

The Captain overflew Scotland's stepping-stone islands
to join a curiosity of seals in their mid-Atlantic gulch.

The seals taught Captain Angel every watery word and
every white wave harmony from the Seal Songbook.

Captain Angel was grateful and rewarded the seals
with sea room, swim-swiftness and the gentlest looks.

Seals still have their sea-power but in recent times
their songs have become gruff, sorrowful – like laments.

Whereas Captain Angel continues to sing the seals'
fabled ocean songs in the opera house of the heavens.

Tra-la-la.

How Captain Angel Learned to Dance

In a day of colour, the colour of seabird feathers,
Captain Angel spotted a clown – not a circus clown,
not a showy, make-uppy, funny-hatty, trouser-baggy
    clown,
but an *angelic* clown, a dancery-mimery clown
whose name was Charlie, simply Charlie.

Captain Angel watched Charlie spin and whirl,
twist and whiz like a cheeky helicopter.
Captain Angel wanted to dance like Charlie
so it was off to the dance studio. It was open on a
    Sunday,
but they did not teach Charlie's kind of dance –
it was (they turned up their noses, sniffed and said)
'too circusy, too clownish'. They only taught
(they looked down their noses, sniffed and said)
'the Twist and the Tango, and the Tootsie-Wootsie
    Tumble.'

So Captain Angel vowed 'I shall teach myself!
I shall dance in a pond of air . . . by next Pancake
    Tuesday.'

Stood in front of the mirror,
practised a Charlie move,
learned Charlie hand-movements,
Charlie kicks and Charlie tricks.
Cried when it didn't work out.

Captain Angel wanted to perform a Charlie dance
for a specially invited audience. Captain Angel painted
on a white face, a black moustache,
       dressed in poor man's
black & white clothes and did a Charlie routine.

The audience applauded, cheered, waved, whistled,
Captain Angel bowed
became beautiful
became better angel,
. . . became bird.

Captain Angel took flight, danced all the way to
       fascination.

Dead Tree at Nightfall

Day's end: a mask of cloud is peeled from the sky
leaving night to set its wide black table.

Stars are gleaming, propped up like tiny plates
in a window in a café in a town in the distant sky.

At the edge of the field behind this house,
a ghost-grey tree stands: jagged, splitting, cracking.

It has stood there, leafless, lifeless, for years –
dead since long before you were born.

In daytime its stark top branches soak up light,
become toeholds for a flutter-and-swoop of pigeons.

But under an ice-blue moon the tree calls alive
its history, tells long-gone stories and adventures.

Once its arms cupped a tree house for local boys;
was dressed on Mayday in streams of coloured ribbons.

Ages back, a rope dangled from its strongest branch
and tightened raw around the neck of a highwayman.

The night a lightning bolt split its trunk revealing
Mad Mary's long-forgotten casket of treasure.

And the arrow wounds in its bark when a battle
raged around this field almost three centuries ago.

Then, at 8 a.m. this morning, two red tractors lashed
wires as thick as arms around its brittle branches.

By quarter past their job was finished –
the chainsaws whirred, the fires crackled.

Across the field, scattering in all directions,
drifted countless words from a wooden history book –

words lost until some storyteller finds them.

On the Laptop of the Little Lambs

On the laptop of the little lambs
it is written:
do not stray too far from your mother,
do not try to squeeze under the fence,
do not go near dogs.

Most cold March mornings
and each Easter in April,
the lambs gather in threes and fours
to power up their laptops
and read these simple instructions,
do not stray too far from your mother,
do not try to squeeze under the fence,
do not go near dogs.

The lambs know
what they should and should not do.
But there's always one that lets things slip
and while the yellow spring sun
tries its quiet best to warm the world,
one lamb wanders off, squeezes under the fence
and meets up with an Alsatian.

Perhaps we need bigger and bolder letters
on the laptop of the little lambs:
do not stray too far from your mother,
do not try to squeeze under the fence,
do not go near dogs.

It's hard to fix a fault in life's software.

Full Frog in a Blue Bucket

Two boys, Charlie and Paddy,
come to the door
in the summer holidays.

They have a full frog
in murky water
at the bottom of a blue bucket.

'It's dead,' says Charlie.
'Doesn't move,' says Paddy.
'Zatzo,' says I.

Charlie won't touch it
but Paddy pokes it with
two of his dirtiest fingers.

Suddenly the frog thrusts out
its back legs, bounds forward
and headbutts the side of the bucket.

Paddy screams, Charlie yells
and both let go
of the blue bucket's handle.

The frog escapes in 'm' shaped bounds
across the road
heading for the stream. (Probably in shock!)

The boys chase after it,
shouting and squealing,
but hardly likely to catch it. (And anyway they're scared
    to touch it.)

I'm left with my trousers and trainers
splattered with stream slime
and a puddle trickling over the doorstep.

I go back indoors to change
and my wife just looks at me,
shakes her head, looks away, and sighs.

Miranda Moon

It was on a warm September day
when we returned to Primary School
after the summer holidays.
Chatting along the road,
some of us with new shoes
some of us with new bags,
some of us holding the hands of tiny brothers or sisters
who were just starting school that day.

Right on 9 o'clock a special assembly was held
and our Head Teacher told the whole school
that Miranda Moon from Mrs Page's class
had been knocked down by a car
when she was on holiday in France.
She had died in hospital a few days later.

The Head Teacher gave us a talk
on how to be careful on the roads
and only play in the ball park where it was safe.
All the children and all the staff
prayed for Miranda Moon.

Miranda Moon was a really kind girl.
She wasn't bossy and she wasn't a show-off.
She wrote excellent poems.
I remember once she read out a poem in class
about our pets and said she loved her dog
'for his big sad eyes, his wiry coat and for his heart,
which was as dark as the inside of our wardrobe'.
That was really good, she was our best writer.

A few days later we all went to church
with our teachers and some of the parents came.
The vicar said more prayers for Miranda.
After that life in school went on as usual really.

But one day, about three weeks later,
when our teacher was reading poems to us
from the school's new anthology,
she read out one of Miranda Moon's poems.
She seemed to read it in a shaky voice.

It was a poem Miranda had written about her granny
and how she had loved her so much
and how much she missed her
since the day she had died of old age.

Our teacher started to cry as she read it
and as she wiped her tears with a tissue
she said to the class
'Look, I just have to go outside
for a moment, please don't make a noise.'

And we didn't . . . all you could
hear was muffled crying and sniffing.

When our teacher came back in
she was smiling and said,
'I think that's one of Miranda's best poems.
Now let's see if we can write one
that talks about how *we* miss *her*.

After that we'd better get some work done
for the Harvest Festival.
Time's marching on you know.'

Going to Secondary
(for Faith)

The summer holidays are almost over.
Everyone's been on holiday
and come back sun-tanned.
Children sleep late then play all day.

Each early morning is misty and chilled,
as if the season has become fed up with
the same old hot days and wants a change.

In just four days time I shall be going
to secondary school.
I have never been as excited as this!

My new uniform hangs in the wardrobe
and every now and again, I wander upstairs
pretending I'm going to read a book or something,
but really I just want to look at my new uniform.

I run my fingers across the yellow
diagonal stripes on my black tie,
or try on my black jacket
(it's just a little too long in the sleeves,
but my mum says it's got to last a few years).
I am really looking forward to putting it on
and walking with my friends to secondary school
in the cool, morning sunshine.

My friends! Of course!
I can't wait to see my friends
in *their* uniforms! No more little
blue jumpers like we wore in primary!
No more boring clothes and shoes with buckles,
we're going to wear slip-ons and the latest fashions.

Only four days to go and I'll be
at secondary school. I feel like the
whole world is hurtling and spinning
and zooming and changing –
and me, little me, I'm right in the middle of it!
What if I get lost in that huge school?
It's vast and maze-like with hundreds
of corridors and classes.
What if I'm late on the very first day – oh no!

Mum says we'll go into town on Monday morning
and get my shoes, and then that's it –
I'll be ready!
(What if they don't have my size?)

I'm so excited and then again,
I'm so nervous and anxious!
Only four more days,
four more days and I'll be
at secondary school.

Say goodbye to childhood for me.

My Favourite Thingummybob

My favourite colour is W,
my favourite drink is bees.
My favourite song is an apple,
and my favourite hat is trees.

My favourite flower is bottle,
my favourite book is socks.
My favourite sweets are 40,
and my favourite game is a fox.

My favourite pet is a teaspoon,
my favourite friend is a clock.
My favourite clothes are biscuits,
and my favourite word is

S
   P
      L
         O
           C
             K
               !

favourite words vol.2

this weeks funniest words.

favourite thingummy bob

trees (small)

gold block drinks

Pressed flowers

most favourite word.

Sulky Silkie*

Tune: 'Suáilcí Samhailcí'

Sulky silkie hi-de-ho
where are you from and where do you go?
Swimming and skimming all through the day,
slubbery blubbery hi-de-hay.

Sulky silkie hi-de-hoo
what do you play and what do you do?
Deep in the ocean cold as can be,
flippery flappery hi-de-hee.

Sulky silkie hi-de-hup
mother seal nuzzles her patchy wee pup.
Huge dark eyes and a whiskery nose,
whiskery tiskery hi-de-hose.

Sulky silkie hi-de-har
you never come close but you never stray far.
A bobbing grey head on the cold water's top,
silkery sulkery hi-de-hop.

Sulky silkie hi-de-hoch
splishing and splashing in the silver sea loch.
I'd watch you all day but it's now time for tea,
finnery finery hi-de-hee.

Sulky silkie hi-de-ho
where you are from and where do you go?
Swimming and skimming all through the day,
sulky silkery hi-de-hay.

*in Scotland a seal is known as a Silkie

Sulky Silkie
(Scots Version)

Sulky silkie hi-di-ho
where are ye frae and whaur dae ye go?
Swimmin' and skimmin' a' through the day,
slubbery blubbery hi-de-hay.

Sulky silkie hi-di-hoo
Whit dae ye play an' whit dae ye do?
Deep in the ocean, cauld as can be,
flippery flappery hi-de-hee.

Sulky silkie hi-di-hup
mither seal nuzzles her patchy wee pup.
Huge dark eyes an' a whiskery nose,
whiskery tiskery hi-de-hose.

Sulky silkie hi-di-har
ye never come close, but ye never stray far.
A bobbin' grey heid on the cauld watter's tap,
silkery sulkery hi-de-hap.

Sulky silkie hi-di-hoch
splishin' an' splashin' aboot in the loch.
Ah'd watch ye a' day, but it's noo time fur tea,
finnery finery hi-de-hee.

Sulky silkie hi-di-ho
where are ye frae and whaur dae ye go?
Swimmin' and skimmin' a' through the day,
sulkery silkery hi-de-hay.

The Could Be, May Be, Then Again Might Not Be, Poem

It was the Day of the Big Porridge
   in the Town of the Ugly Babies.
There were several well perhapses
   and quite a few ach maybes.

The wind it may have been blowing
   and the sun was possibly shining.
Sail boats could well have been sailing
   and some miners might've been mining.

Clouds dithered all day about drifting
   with trees disinclined to sway.
And perhaps a duck was diving
   on this very improbable day.

Sparrows were faced with decisions,
   whether breadcrumbs or bacon rinds.
And comparative logic professors
   couldn't make up their minds.

Cats thought twice about sleeping,
  dogs wondered whether to yawn.
And the clock took its time about ticking;
  we'll be lucky to ever see dawn.

It was the Night of the Straggly Tassels
  in the City of Size 9 Boot.
There were several well it could be's,
  but, no one gave a hoot!

History Lesson: The Romans

All over their Empire
the Romans built impressive buildings
such as forts, villas and monuments.
In big cities they constructed huge *Amphitheatres*
where great games and spectacles were held.

The best known of these
are the Roman Games with contests,
often the death, between animals,
between men and between women combatants.

It was in one of these amphitheatres
that Miranda, the wife of Emperor Tiberius Tempus,
accidentally fell from her balcony into the arena
and was attacked and eaten by a tiger.

The tiger was told off and sent to bed.
Everyone agreed it was bad he ate her,
the Emperor was sad he ate her,
poor old Miranda was mad he ate her,
but the tiger said she was tasty and he was
GLADIATOR!

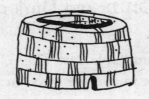

The Boy Who Was Nearly Swallowed Up
by the Cupboard Under the Stairs

In those long, unfillable days after Christmas,
when parents lie in and the days slow down
to cloud passing pace,
a boy came home from the football field
muddied and red-faced, hot and wearing
too many clothes, having misjudged the temperature.

Into the kitchen to grab a swig of drink
and a doorstep cheese sandwich –
the studs of his football boots
clacking and slipping on the tiled floor
and leaving a trail of mud and grass
that would look perfect for
a floor-cleaner advert set-design.

'Get that ball off the kitchen table
and get those boots off right now – outside!'
He kind of expected this yelled double demand,
so it came as no surprise.
In fact he was already making
his way to the back door.

Football in hand and in stocking soles,
he sockboarded across the kitchen floor
spreading the muck like an abstract in Tate Modern.

Into the hall and open the latch
on the cupboard under the stairs
(tight as a muscle man's bathroom tap!)
– and there's this little sound,
not quite a catcall, not quite a dog-yawn,
not quite an animal and certainly not a baby.

Dark in there, the only light-coloured thing
is the hoover and even it's partly covered with
        raincoats.
He tries to throw the football in, any-old-where.
But it falls back out, in fact is thrown back out.
So he tries placing it.
Placing it on top of the pile of shoes,
but it doesn't take hold, just rolls off.

And then, sounding like an orchestra careering into
        chaos,
there's a shout from the kitchen, something falls
on the landing making a great crashing noise,
without warning the dog jumps on his back
almost pushing him into the cupboard
so he shoves the ball in between the fleeces, overcoats
and sports jackets. Shoves it hard as he can
with fright jellifying his arms.

And something in there, something unseen but
        mumbling
grabs both the ball and his wrists.
Something clammy and damp.
It won't let go no matter how hard he tugs and jerks.
And it seems it wants to yank him into this dark,
        musty world
where darkness and stuffiness are ever present;
from where there is no escape,
from where no light emerges,
and where terror grows in its birth-nest.

The Machine of the Three Big Ears

LISA, the Laser Interferometer Space Antenna, will be launched in 2008 and is intended to prove the existence of 'sounds in space'

Only part of me is metal,
only part of me is fibreglass,
for I am nothing but
a triangle of ears.

And high in the heavens,
motionless and steady,
my Three Big Ears will listen
for the waterless waves that rise and fall
across the oceans of space.

By star, by day, throughout the years
of your childhood, your adulthood,
I shall be listening for those waves
with my Three Big Ears,
my no head, my no body, my no legs,
millions of miles apart,
connected by laser beam.
my nothing but Three Big Ears connected
as you grow in body and brain.

What shall I listen for
with my Three Big Ears?

For the singing of the supernova,
for the ringing of runaway stars,
for the plug-hole suck of black holes,
for the chirrup of galaxies colliding.

And, reader, in your old age,
you will think of my Three Big Ears
catching the tiny tinkling sounds of space
and catapulting them to Earth,
to the Two Small Ears
on your curious body machine.

The Mysterious Object in
the Bathroom

Come closer! I'll whisper.

I don't know if you've seen it
but there's something mysterious
in the bathroom.
I'm not sure what it is
or what it's for.

It just sits there in a little puddle
of water at the side of the washbasin.
It's white, oval-shaped and has a flowery smell.
My little brother has no idea what it is either.
He says it could be a white toffee bar –
But I don't fancy eating it.

Sometimes when you go in there
it sort of glistens as if it has been in water.
Other times it's bone dry. Very strange.
One day I'll find out what this white bar is for.
Maybe it has something to do with that long
brush that has bristles at the end of it –
you know, the one I use for getting the mud
out of my studs after football.

Merry Confusemix

Weather crackling.
Sleigh bells humming.
Vicar twinkling.
Robins praying.
Frost photographing.
Holly heating.
Slippers glowing.
Logs glinting.
Candles ringing.
Tinsel playing.
Angels baa-ing.
Santa snoring.
Music unwrapping.
Computers smiling.
Dogs dancing.
Stockings watching.
Presents visiting.
Dad crumbling.
Mince pies dangling.
Grandma barking.
Carol singers shining.

Mulled wine yawning.
Stars warming.
Shepherds hanging.
Sheep flying.
Biscuits raining.
Turkey singing.
Pudding hopping.
House burning.
Children cooking.

The Hungry Wolf

The hungry wolf
      is very wild
and is guaranteed
      to devour a child.

So do take care
      if a wolf's about,
and if you fancy chips,
      send your sister out!

Water Daughter

I have a new friend
   on a Scottish riverbank.
She catches little fish
   in places damp and dank.

Her long stiff hair
   makes a waterproof coat,
and with her agile swimming
   she's like a fast patrol boat.

Her jaws are very strong,
   her habitat is watery.
I won her last week
   in the National Ottery.

The Shepherd and His Daughter

(for Gordon Giltrap)

Deep in the West Highlands, among mountains,
a narrow one-track road, a purposeful road,
crosses the rushing, chattering waters of the River Polly.

Along this road hobbles a squabble of sheep.
They are being ushered along
by silent, tireless collie dogs under orders.
It is a down moon; it is an empty sun.

The shepherd walks along behind the flock
gripping a tall crook in his right hand.
It was his father's crook, and his father's before that.

He lightly holds his child daughter's hand in his left.
She is perhaps three, perhaps four.
Bouncy. Elfin. Riverish.

She wears the brightest raggle-taggle clothes:
pale pink cardy, multi-coloured skirt, blue wellies.
The imprisoned sheep are off-white.

The shepherd's eyes are fixed on the road ahead.
He walks purposefully, orders the dogs
with shrill whistles and sharp commands.

Her blue wellies slopping in puddles,
the daughter skips and trips along,
singing a who-knows-which song.

Now and forever on,
her father minds the sheep, minds her.

In time, the road and the river become one.

Two Ghosts

Just before dawn goes on duty,
she throws open our bedroom door,
shakes me, wakes me.

'I dreamt that every day,
when I wasn't there,
a little teddy walked about
under my bed. When I came in,
it fell over and stopped walking.'

At first it all sounded logical,
since I myself thought
this was all a dream.
But her shaky voice is full of worry
and I know why she's here,
the night is so big.

We go downstairs to talk
of god and ghosts and dead things.
She sips Coca-Cola, I drink Lucozade
(hoping to avoid being one of the
dead things too soon!)

After a time we return to our beds.
In the brightening morning
we glide upstairs –
we look like our own ghosts.

I skim her cheek with a kiss,
saying, 'Go back to sleep now.'
I feel pleased that I have
brushed away her cares and worries
with a father's reassurance.

'Yes,' she answers, 'but first I'll have
just one more look under the bed.'

The Garden of Greatness

(for Therese Eklund)

Deep in a north country, far from the coast,
it is the last of winter and the first of summer.

A hungry bird, a fieldfare, flies over the river;
he skims a wooden fence and lands inside
the Garden of Greatness.

We follow, unseen.

Look. The ice has melted but the gardener
still wears her scarf (crocus coloured).
The sun is new-born bright so the gardener
wears a light shirt (white as salt).
She will always know star-cold, earth-warmth.

Listen. There is a quietness, a brown softness
about the Garden of Greatness.
The speech of insects is hushed
and the birds tilt their heads to whisper.
A garden fire fades in the far corner, hissing.

The Garden is like a tiny churchyard of silence
as butterflies soundlessly tramp across flowers,
pond fish burble tales of their watery travels
('I once saw a swallow asleep on the sea bed!')
The bee-keeper hums inside his yellow helmet.
Marigolds and magpies chatter about
the cattle-shed that once stood here.

For centuries gone, and for centuries to come,
the Garden of Greatness will grow many names.
Names that are nearly green, and strong as stone.
Names that huddle around a kingdom of nature
to cook a bubbling word-soup of
dust, stone, bark, bone, leaf, weed, earth, seed –

a gathering of guests for the plants' wedding.

Teddies can be Ferocious Creatures

I've been thinking a lot about teddies,
   the soft and cuddly kind.
Truth is, a real one could eat you –
   please Grizzly bear that in mind.

Nice School Photo

In all the schools,
in all the country,
in all the world,
there are photographers
making us look like everyone else.

'Very nice, nice smile now,
very nice, nice photo for your granny,
just say cheese'

Same backdrop,
same kind of school uniform,
same bright-eyed smile,
same head, same freckles, same shoulders,
same slight angle, same pose,
same skin tones from the same lighting,
same school, same town, same face,
same nose, same ears, same cheeks,
same this, same that, same . . . same . . . same
SAME CHILD!

'Very nice, nice smile now,
very nice, nice photo for your granny,
just say cheese'

But I'm me!
I don't look like my friends, I look different!

Next time we have a school photo taken
I'm going to wear a gorilla mask,
a smuggler's eye patch, Dracula teeth,
a Santa beard, a cowboy hat
and stick a baby's dummy in my mouth.

'Very nice, nice smile now,
very nice, nice photo for your granny,
oh you do look a little different from the other children'

Yes, my parents always wanted a
smuggling scary baby gorilla cowboy Father Christmas
who looked like all the others.

'Hmm, that's nice,
just say cheese'

The Stick Insects in the Museum

Saturday evening, just on 5 p.m.
The Library and Museum
are about to close.

Most of us are at home,
football scores on the television,
tea on the table.

The museum curator secures the strong lid
on the glass case containing the stick insects
in their never-blue world.

Everyone will be busy tomorrow
only six more shopping days
before Christmas.

The stick insects won't be busy.
They will remain motionless in their
greeny-brown camouflage – all night, all day.

On Saturday night
families will go to the local pantomime,
grandparents to carol concerts, teenagers to parties.

During the drowsiness of Sunday,
one stick insect might, just might,
twist her twig-like body one single centimetre.

By Monday it's up early again,
back to work, back to school
for just a few more days before the holiday.

At 8.30 a.m., the museum curator unlocks
the door to the Library and Museum
and walks through the still, hushed foyer.

She finds one stick insect, in the shape of
an exclamation mark, crawling downstairs
heading for the exit.

Caribbean Carnival Cavalcade

Face-painted folk start the celebrations,
  carnival is here so congratulations.
Festive fun and jubilations,
  so skim along friend, get in circulation!
  Watch out for *balloons and booms*
            whooshes and zooms
            steel-pan play
            on a sundance day
            balls and whoops
            clowns fall, whoops!
            red-nosed faces
            playing catch and chases.

Teddy-bear girls and puppet-show boys,
  a day of laughter, cheers and noise.
Yo-yoing dads are playing with toys,
  dancing mums in clown convoys!
  Here come the *poppers and streamers*
            pop-song screamers
            comics and cakes
            slimy trick snakes
            limbo dancers
            rocking-horse prancers
            banjos and bingo
            badges by jingo!

Lipsticked lips, a painted face,
    coconut shies and a skipping race.
Dress up as a nurse or a monster from space,
    joy and fun are commonplace!
    Let's see some *skylark pranks*
                robot clanks
                leapfrog razzles
                sunshine dazzles
                circus mime
                busker time
                slapstick fun
                mara-fun run
                people at play
                on Caribbean
                    Carnival
                        Cavalcade day!!!

THE WORKS

Every kind of poem
you will ever need for the
Literacy Hour

Chosen by Paul Cookson

The Works really does contain every kind of poem *you* will ever need for the Literacy Hour, but it is *also* a book packed with brilliant poems that *will* delight any reader.

It's got chants, action verses, riddles, tongue-twisters, shape poems, puns, acrostics, haikus, cinquains, kennings, couplets, thin poems, lists, conversations, monologues, epitaphs, songs, limericks, tankas, nonsense poems, raps, narrative verse and performance poetry, and that's just for starters!

*It features poems from the very best classical
and modern poets,
for example:*

*William Blake, Michael Rosen, Robert Louis Stevenson,
Allan Ahlberg, W. H. Auden, Brian Patten, Roger McGough,
Roald Dahl, Charles Causley, Eleanor Farjeon,
Benjamin Zephaniah, Ted Hughes, T. S. Eliot, and
William Shakespeare, to name but a few.*

**A book packed with gems for dipping into time
and time again.**